THE LANGUAGE OF...

RUGBY

The rugby enthusiast's phrasebook in 5 languages

with illustrations by Clive Collins

Rugby is now played across the world from Scotland to South Africa, from Japan to South America. The Language of Rugby is the ideal companion to this truly international sport, containing all the phrases and vocabulary needed for most situations with translations into the most useful of rugby languages: Afrikaans, French, Italian, Spanish and Welsh. The Spanish translation of the phrases is in Latin American Spanish as rugby is more developed in Latin America (especially in Argentina and Uruguay) than in Spain. Some terms do not have direct translations whilst others vary according to whether the French or the British introduced the game to the country. Since the game is originally British we have used English terminology where no translation is available.

THE TRY

'If the ball's in there, it's a try'.

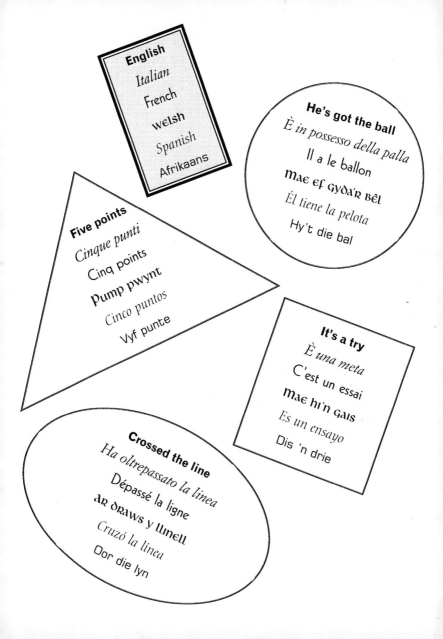

English
Italian
French
welsh
Spanish
Afrikaans

He's got the ball
È in possesso della palla
Il a le ballon
ᴍᴀᴇ ᴇf ɢʏᴅᴀ'ʀ ʙêʟ
Él tiene la pelota
Hy't die bal

Five points
Cinque punti
Cinq points
Pump pwynt
Cinco puntos
Vyf punte

It's a try
È una meta
C'est un essai
ᴍᴀᴇ ʜɪ'ɴ ɢᴀɪs
Es un ensayo
Dis 'n drie

Crossed the line
Ha oltrepassato la linea
Dépassé la ligne
ᴀʀ ᴅʀᴀws ʏ ʟʟɪɴᴇʟʟ
Cruzó la línea
Oor die lyn

THE GOAL POSTS

'It's that new groundsman - we should have specified a <u>capital</u> H.'

Wait for the crowd's roar
Aspetta il clamore della folla
Attendre les rugissements
de la foule
ARHOSEWCH Y RHU O'R
GROWD
Espera el gritó de la multitud
Wag vir die skare se gejuig

Through the posts
Attraverso i pali
Entre les poteaux
tRWY'R PYSTS
Por entre los palos
Deur die pale

It's the new groundsman
È il nuovo assistente di campo
C'est le nouveau gardien du stade
Y DDYN DDEUAR NEWYDD
Es el nuevo encargado de la cancha
Dis die nuwe ou wat die veld versorg

He just pushed it wide
Ha fatto un lancio largo
Il vient de le tirer à l'extérieur
MAE EF WEDI GWITHO I'R OCHR
La acaba de tirar afuera
Hy't wyd geskop

THE RUCK/MAUL

'Can someone tell the ref that this ruck is very definitely stationary.'

A rolling maul

Una maul

Un maul pénétrant

SGARRUS THROI

Una formacion movil

'N Rolskrum

Watch out for stamping

Attento a non essere calpestato

Attention au piétinement

Gosfalwch am stampio

Cuidado con los pisotones

Pasop vir trap

This is nothing compared to...!

Questo è niente in confronto a...!

Ce n'est rien comparé à...!

Does dim fel i...!

¡Esto no es nada comparado con...!

Dis niks in vergelyking met...!

Diving over the top

Gettarsi sul mucchio

Plonger par dessus

Yn deifio dras y phen

Se zambulle sobre

Bo-oor geduik

THE SCRUM

'They got fed up with being penalised for collapsing the scrum.'

Five yard scrum
Mischia di 5 yarde
Mêlée à cinq
Scrwm pum lath
Scrum cinco
Vyf tree-skrum

**It's
Wales' put in**
*Rimessa in gioco
del Galles*
Introduction au Pays de Galles
Gymru i ddodi mewn
Gales tira la pelota en el scrum
Wallis moet ingooi

Foul, scrum to France
Fallo, mischia alla Francia
Faute, mêlée pour la France
amfadwaith, scrwm i ffrainc
Falta, scrum para Francia
Fout, Franse se skrum

**They're going
for the pushover try**
Vogliono fare una pushover try
Ils vont essayer de marquer un essai en
poussant la mêlée
mae nhw mynd am gais gwthiod
Van a hacer un try de scrum
Hulle gaan vir 'n oordruk-drie

THE CONVERSION

'I know it's a shame but we need the 3 points!'

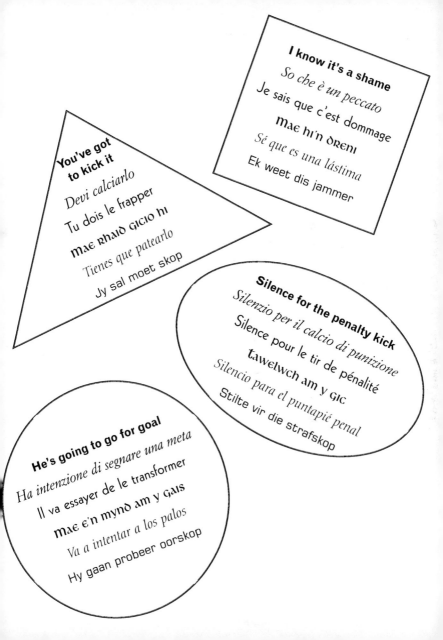

I know it's a shame
So che è un peccato
Je sais que c'est dommage
ᴍᴀᴇ ʜɪ'ɴ ᴅʀᴇɴɪ
Sé que es una lástima
Ek weet dis jammer

You've got to kick it
Devi calciarlo
Tu dois le frapper
ᴍᴀᴇ ʀʜᴀɪᴅ ɢɪᴄɪᴏ ʜɪ
Tienes que patearlo
Jy sal moet skop

Silence for the penalty kick
Silenzio per il calcio di punizione
Silence pour le tir de pénalité
ᴛᴀᴡᴇʟᴡᴄʜ ᴀᴍ ʏ ɢɪᴄ
Silencio para el puntapié penal
Stilte vir die strafskop

He's going to go for goal
Ha intenzione di segnare una meta
Il va essayer de le transformer
ᴍᴀᴇ ᴇ'ɴ ᴍʏɴᴅ ᴀᴍ ʏ ɢᴀɪs
Va a intentar a los palos
Hy gaan probeer oorskop

THE LINE-OUT

'I wish you'd told us before selection that you haven't got a head for heights.'

A little trick they perfected

Un trucchetto che hanno perfezionato

Un petit truc qu'ils ont travaillé

ᵭric mae nhw weᵭi gwneuᵭ

Un pequeño truco que perfeccionaron

'N Kunsie wat hulle vervolmaak het

Queue-jumping

Non rispettare la coda

Resquiller

ℕeiᵭio'r ciw

Colarse

Wag nie sy beurt af nie

Two-man line-out

Rimessa laterale a 2

Touche entre deux

llinell dau ᵭᵭyn

Salida lateral de dos hombres

Tweeman-lynstaan

Line-out on Scotland's twenty two

Rimessa laterale sulla linea dei 22 metri della Scozia

Touche dans les vingt deux écossais

llinell ar ochr daw ᵭᵭeg dau yr alban

Salida lateral en las veintidós de Escocia

Lynstaan op Skotland se 22 meter

THE REFEREE

'...don't try that innocent look with me!'

That innocent look doesn't fool me

Quello sguardo innocente non mi inganna

Ce regard innocent ne prend pas avec moi

mae'r wynet diniwed ddim yn weithio arnaf fi

No me engañas con esa mirada inocente

Daai onskuldige kyk bluf my nie

The ref has called the captains over

L'arbitro ha convocato i capitani

L'arbitre a appelé les capitaines

mae'r dyfarnwr wedi alw y ddau gapten draw

El árbitro llamó a los capitanes

Die skeidsregter het die kapteins geroep

Yellow/red card

Cartellino giallo/rosso

Carton jaune/rouge

Cardeu melyn/coch

Tarjeta amarilla/roja

Geel kaart/rooi kaart

Consulting the touch judge

Consultare il giudice di touche

Consulter l'arbitre de touche

Yn ymgynghori gyda'r barnwyr

Consultando al juez de línea

Raadpleeg die grensregter

THE DRESS CODE

'He says he doesn't want to end up looking like me.'

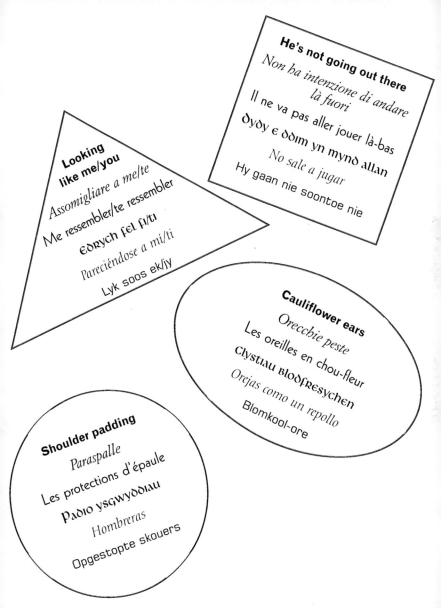

He's not going out there
Non ha intenzione di andare là fuori
Il ne va pas aller jouer là-bas
ᵭyᵭy e ᵭᵭim yn mynᵭ allan
No sale a jugar
Hy gaan nie soontoe nie

Looking like me/you
Assomigliare a me/te
Me ressembler/te ressembler
Edrych fel fi/ti
Pareciéndose a mi/ti
Lyk soos ek/jy

Cauliflower ears
Orecchie peste
Les oreilles en chou-fleur
Clystiau blodfresychen
Orejas como un repollo
Blomkool-ore

Shoulder padding
Paraspalle
Les protections d'épaule
Padio ysgwyddiau
Hombreras
Opgestopte skouers

THE PROPS

'I feel just like a rose between two thorns...'

A rose between two thorns

Una rosa tra due spine

Une rose entre deux épines

Rhosyn rhwng ddau ddraenen

Una nena entre dos bestias

'N Roos tussen twee dorings

Tight-head prop

*Pilone schierato
alla destra del tallonatore
nella prima fila della mischia*

Pilier droit

Yr rheng flaen

Pilar cerrado

Vaskop-stut

Loose-head prop

*Pilone che si posiziona a lato
del suo mediano di mischia*

Pilier gauche

Yr rheng flaen

Pilar abierto

Loskop-stut

Front-row forwards

Prime linee

Première ligne

Blaen rhes ymlaen

*Primera linea,
pilares y hooker*

Voorry

THE HOOKER

'"Handbags at ten paces" is just an expression, Gordon.'

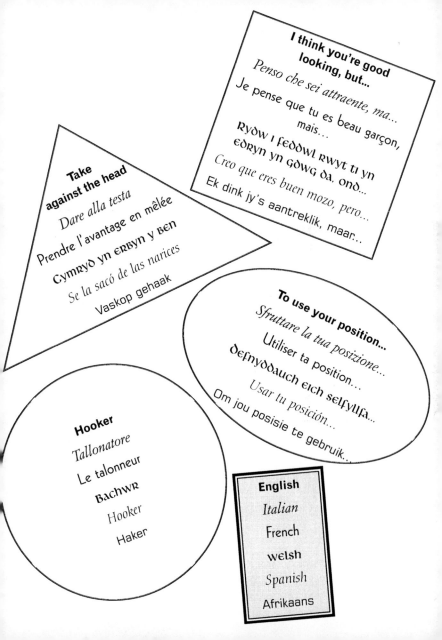

I think you're good looking, but...

Penso che sei attraente, ma...

Je pense que tu es beau garçon, mais...

Rydw i feddwl rwyt ti yn edryn yn gowg da, ond...

Creo que eres buen mozo, pero...

Ek dink jy's aantreklik, maar...

Take against the head

Dare alla testa

Prendre l'avantage en mêlée

Cymryd yn erbyn y ben

Se la sacó de las narices

Vaskop gehaak

To use your position...

Sfruttare la tua posizione...

Utiliser ta position...

Defnyddauch eich selfyllfa...

Usar tu posición...

Om jou posisie te gebruik...

Hooker

Tallonatore

Le talonneur

Bachwr

Hooker

Haker

English

Italian

French

welsh

Spanish

Afrikaans

THE LOCKS

'A slight problem, lads - we've had a complaint from air traffic control.'

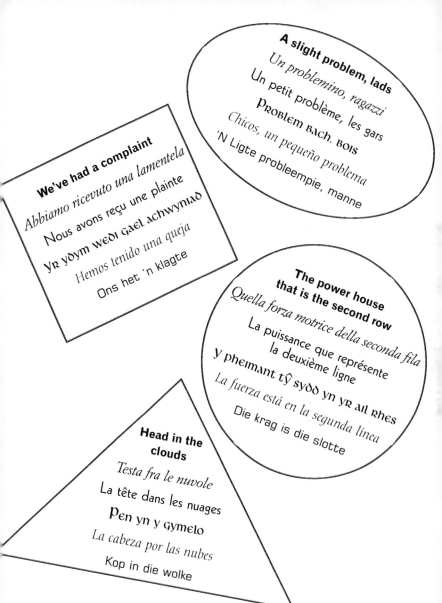

A slight problem, lads
Un problemino, ragazzi
Un petit problème, les gars
ᴘʀᴏʙʟᴇᴍ ʙᴀᴄʜ, ʙᴏɪꜱ
Chicos, un pequeño problema
'N Ligte probleempie, manne

We've had a complaint
Abbiamo ricevuto una lamentela
Nous avons reçu une plainte
ʏʀ ʏᴅʏᴍ ᴡᴇᴅɪ ɢᴀᴇʟ ᴀᴄʜᴡʏɴɪᴀᴅ
Hemos tenido una queja
Ons het 'n klagte

**The power house
that is the second row**
Quella forza motrice della seconda fila
La puissance que représente
la deuxième ligne
ʏ ᴘʜᴇɪᴍᴀɴᴛ ᴛŷ ꜱʏᴅᴅ ʏɴ ʏʀ ᴀɪʟ ʀʜᴇꜱ
La fuerza está en la segunda línea
Die krag is die slotte

**Head in the
clouds**
Testa fra le nuvole
La tête dans les nuages
ᴘᴇɴ ʏɴ ʏ ɢʏᴍᴇʟᴏ
La cabeza por las nubes
Kop in die wolke

THE BACK ROW

'Surely we don't have to stay bound after the ball's gone?'

The back row forwards
Le seconde linee centro
La troisième ligne
Y Rhes Gefen
La tercera línea
Skrum vorentoe

Glamour position
Posizione "in"
La position en vogue
Safle Dliwgar
Posición ideal
Spog-posisie

Open side/blind side Flanker
Lato aperto/Lato chiuso
Flanker côté ouvert/côté fermé
Blaenasgell ochor agoredd/ochor diwedd
Flanker abierto/del lado ciego
Oop flanke/toe flanke

Number eight
Il numero otto
Le numéro huit
Dyn Rhif wyth
El octavo
Die agtste man

THE SCRUM-HALF

'Don't you just hate it when they do that?'

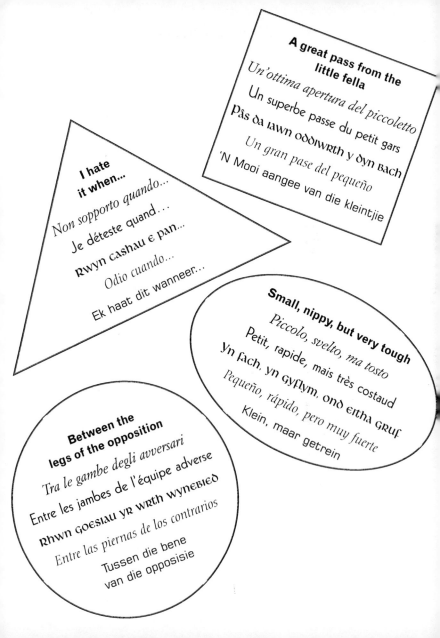

A great pass from the little fella

Un'ottima apertura del piccoletto

Un superbe passe du petit gars

Pâs da iawn oddiwrth y dyn bach

Un gran pase del pequeño

'N Mooi aangee van die kleintjie

I hate it when...

Non sopporto quando...

Je déteste quand...

Rwyn cashau e pan...

Odio cuando...

Ek haat dit wanneer...

Small, nippy, but very tough

Piccolo, svelto, ma tosto

Petit, rapide, mais très costaud

Yn fach, yn gyflym, ond eitha gruf

Pequeño, rápido, pero muy fuerte

Klein, maar getrein

Between the legs of the opposition

Tra le gambe degli avversari

Entre les jambes de l'équipe adverse

Rhwn Goesiau yr wrth wynebied

Entre las piernas de los contrarios

Tussen die bene van die opposisie

THE FLY-HALF

'He might <u>think</u> a good game...
but I wonder how good he is on his feet?'

Quick hands
Mani svelte
Mains agiles
ꝺwylio ɢyflym
Manos rápidas
Vinnige hande

The feet of a dancer
I piedi di un ballerino
Les pieds d'un danseur
ꞇꞃaeꝺ ꝺꝺawnswiꞃ
Los pies de un bailarín
Die voete van 'n danseres

The playmaker
Il playmaker
Le demi d'ouverture
y ꝺꝺyn chwaꞃae
El armador
Bepaler van spelpatroon

He's brainy enough
Di cervello ne ha abbastanza
Il est suffisamment malin
mae e'n ꝺꝺiɢon siaꞃp
Es suficientemente listo
Hy't 'n goeie kop

THE WINGERS

'This mud is going to absolutely ruin your manicure...'

The flying winger

L'ala volante

L'ailier volant

Y asgell cyflym

El alero veloz

Die vlieënde vleuel

**This mud is going
to ruin your manicure**

Questo fango ti rovinerà la manicure

Cette boue va ruiner ta manucure

Mae'r llaes yn mynd i striwa'r ddiwlo

Este barro te va a arruinar la manicura

Kyk hoe vuil maak
die modder jou naeltjies

The pretty boys

Le femminucce

Les jolis garçons

Y bechgyn pert

Los chicos lindos

Die mooi outjies

I think I've got a splinter

*Penso di avere
una scheggia*

Je pense que j'ai une épine

Rydwi'n meddwl mae brugen gen i

Creo que tengo una astilla

Ek dink ek het 'n splinter opgetel

THE FULL-BACK

'When he's called for the mark - let's make sure we both leave one.'

Calling for the mark

Chiedere il "mark"

Crier mark

Galw am y fare

Pidiendo marca

Merk gevang

He's under the Garryowen

E in ricezione di un up-and-under

Il est sous la chandelle

Mae o'n dan y Garryowen

Está bajo una pelota colgada

Hy's onder die hoë skop

A great tackle by the last man

Un ottimo passaggio da parte dell'ultimo uomo

Un superbe tackle du dernier homme

Tacl mawr gan y ddyn diwethaf

Un gran tackle del último hombre

'N Mooi vat deur die laaste man

The full-back joins the line at pace

Il tre quarti estremo si allinea in velocità

L' arrière rejoint la ligne d'attaque à toute vitesse

Mae'r dy diwethaf yn gwrdd a'r llinell yn gyflym

El full-back se pliega a la línea a tiempo

Die heelagter sluit hom op spoed aan

HALF-TIME

'I can't hear what he's saying either, but it seems to involve a four-letter word.'

He uses sign language well

È bravo con il linguaggio dei segni

Il se sert bien du langage des signes

Mae e yn defwyddio iaith law hefyd

Él se maneja bien con el lenguaje por señas

Hy's goed met vingertaal

I can't hear a word he's saying

Non sento una parola di quello che dice

Je n'entend pas un mot de ce qu'il dit

Rydw i ddim yn gallu lywed gaer mae e'n wneud

No le escucho ni una palabra de lo que dice

Ek kan g'n woord hoor wat hy sê nie

Half-time talk

Discorso fatto nell'intervallo

Discussion de la mi-temps

Siariad rhen hanner amser

Entretiempo

Rustyd-praatjie

The team coach

L'allenatore della squadra

L'entraîneur de l'équipe

Yr gwedd hyfforddwr

El entrenador del equipo

Die span-afrigter

THE KIT

'I knew that starting a minis section
would lead to problems'

It's all we've got

È tutto ciò che abbiamo

C'est tout ce que nous avons

ꝺyna ᵹyꝺ syꝺꝺ ᵹyꝺa nı

Es todo lo que tenemos

Dis al wat ons het

Perhaps nobody will notice

Magari nessuno ci farà caso

Peut-être que personne ne se rendra compte

ɛꝼyllau welyꝼꝼ neℬ

Tal vez nadie se dará cuenta

Miskien sien niemand dit

Shirts are available in the club shop

Le maglie sono disponibili nel negozio della squadra

Des maillots dont disponibles dans le magasin du club

ꞽae crꞽsꞽau amwerth yn sꞽop y ᵹlwℬ

Hay camisetas en la tienda del club

Truie is in die klubwinkel te kry

The official team kit

L'uniforme ufficiale della squadra

Le kit officiel de l'équipe

yr ꝺꞽllaꝺ tîm swyꝺꝺoᵹol

La indumentaria oficial del equipo

Die amptelike spantoerusting

THE WINNERS

'Of course I'm proud of them winning - but why couldn't
they do all that sort of thing with cheap Muscadet?'

**I'm proud
of them winning**

Sono orgoglioso della loro vittoria

Je suis fier qu'ils aient gagné

ʀwyn ʙlɛs ʙoᴅ nhw wɛᴅɪ ennɪll

Estoy orgulloso de que ganaran

Ek is trots op hul
oorwinning

We are the Champions

Siamo i campioni

Nous sommes les champions

nɪ yw'ʀ ennɪll wɪʀ

Somos los campeones

Ons is die Kampioene

**They'll be dancing
in the streets tonight**

Stasera balleranno per le strade

Ce soir il vont danser dans les rues

ʙyᴅᴅ nhw'n ᴅawnsɪo yn y sᴛʀyᴅaeᴅᴅ heno

Esta noche estarán bailando en las calles

Hulle gaan vanaand in die strate dans

**There can
only be one winner**

*Ci puó essere
solo un vincitore*

Il ne peut y avoir qu'un gagnant

maɛ ɢallɛ ʙoᴅ onᴅ un enɪllwʀ

Sólo puede haber un ganador

Daar kan net een wenner wees

THE LOSERS

'All I said was 'it's not the winning - it's the taking part'...'

Runners up

Secondi in classifica

Les seconds

ʏ ᴄᴏʟʟᴡʀ

Segundos

Tweede gekom

All I said...

Ho solo detto...

Tout ce que j'ai dit...

ʏ ɢʏᴅ ʏʀ ᴏᴇᴅᴅᴡɴ ɪ ᴡᴇᴅɪ ᴅᴡᴀᴇᴜᴅ...

Sólo dije...

Al wat ek gesê het...

It's not the winning, it's the taking part

L'importante non è vincere, è partecipare

Ce qui compte c'est de participer, pas de gagner

ᴍᴀᴇ ᴇ ᴅᴅɪᴍ ʏʀ ᴇɴɪʟʟ ᴏɴʏ ᴄʏᴍʀʏᴅ ʀʜᴀɴ

Lo importante no es ganar sino competir

Dit gaan nie oor wen nie, maar om deel te neem

In the end, they weren't good enough

In fin dei conti non sono stati abbastanza bravi

Tout compte fait ils n'étaient pas assez bons

ʏɴ ʏʀ ᴅɪᴡᴇᴅᴅ ʏʀ ᴏᴇᴅᴅʜᴡʏɴᴛ ᴅᴅɪᴍ ᴅɪɢᴏɴ ᴅᴀ

Al final no eran suficientemente buenos

Op die ou end was hulle net nie goed genoeg nie

THE TACKLE

'All I said was that I thought the Haka looked a bit poofy'

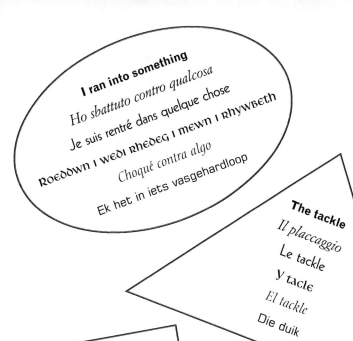

I ran into something
Ho sbattuto contro qualcosa
Je suis rentré dans quelque chose
Roeddwn i wedi rhedeg i mewn i rhywbeth
Choqué contra algo
Ek het in iets vasgehardloop

The tackle
Il placcaggio
Le tackle
Y tacle
El tackle
Die duik

Ambulance-men
I soccorritori
Les ambulanciers
Dyn ambilwns
Los enfermeros
Ambulans-manne

Stretcher-bearers
Barellieri
Les brancardiers
Cludwyr elorwely
Camilleros
Die draagbaar-ouens

THE PHYSIO

'No, no, really - it's just a scratch - the pain's going off now, I can hardly feel a thing!'

It's just a scratch

È solo un graffio

C'est seulement une égratignure

ᵯᴀᴇ ɛ ᴆᴆɪᴍ ᴏᴎᴆ ᴄʀᴀғɪᴀᴆ

Es sólo un rasguño

Dis net 'n skrapie

The pain's going now

Adesso il dolore è passato

La douleur s'en va maintenant

ᵯᴀᴇ'ʀ ᴘᴏᴇᴎ ʏᴎ ᴍʏᴎᴆ ᴎᴀᴡʀ

Ya no me duele

Dit voel nou beter

He's picked up a nasty knock

Si è preso un brutto colpo

Il s'est fait une vilaine blessure

ᵯᴀᴇ ɛ ᴡᴇᴆɪ ᴄᴏᴆɪ ʟᴀᴎ ᴄᴎᴏᴄ ɢᴀs

Se lastimó bastante

Hy het 'n sleg besering

He'll need treatment for that

Dovrà farselo curare

Il va avoir besoin de soins

ʙʏᴆᴆᴇᴎ ᴇsɪᴀᴜ ᴛʀɪᴍᴀᴇᴛʜ ᴀʀ ʜᴡᴎᴎᴀ

Necesitará tratamiento para eso

Hy sal behandeling daarvoor moet kry

THE COMMUNAL BATH

'Hold it chaps, Bruno thinks the opposition scrum-half
might be in here somewhere.'

The communal bath
I *bagni comuni*
Le bain commun
Y ʙᴀᴛʜ cyfunol
La bañadera común
Die gesamentlike bad

Pass the soap
Passa la saponetta
Passe(z)-moi le savon
Pᴀsɪwɪᴄʜ y sᴇʙᴀɴ
Pásame el jabón
Gee die seep aan

I don't want to worry anyone
Non voglio allarmare nessuno
Je ne veux inquiéter personne
Rwy ᴆᴆɪᴍ ᴇsɪᴀᴜ cynʜʀfɪɴᴇʙ
No quiero preocupar a nadie
Ek wil nie pla nie

**Bruno has
lost his rubber duck**
*Bruno ha perso
la paperetta di plastica*
Bruno a perdu son canard en plastique
ᴍᴀᴇ ʙʀᴜɴo weᴆɪ ᴄoʟʟɪ ᴇɪ ʜwyᴀᴆ ʀʜwʙʀᴀɴ
Bruno ha perdido su patito de goma
Bruno het sy eendjie verloor

THE INTERVIEW

'Shall I take that as 'no comment'?'

No comment

No comment

Sans commentaire

ðim esboniað

Sin comentarios

Geen kommentaar

The post match interview

L'intervista dopo la partita

L' interview de fin du match

y cyfarfyddiad gorffenol a'r oll y match

La entrevista al final del partido

Die onderhoud ná die wedstryd

The lads played well

I ragazzi hanno giocato bene

Les gars ont bien joué

Maer bechgyn yn chwarae yn ðða

Los chicos jugaron bien

Die manne het goed gespeel

English

Italian

French

welsh

Spanish

Afrikaans

Can we just have a quick word?

Possiamo scambiare due parole?

Pouvons-nous parler une minute?

Gallwn ni cael gair gyflym?

¿Podemos hablar un minuto?

Kan ons 'n woordjie kry?

THE PLAYERS' DIET

'He has to be careful - apparently this sort of diet goes straight to his thighs.'

He has to be careful

Deve fare attenzione

Il doit faire attention

Mae en ɢᴏʀꜰᴏᴅ ʙᴏᴅ yn ofalus

Tiene que tener cuidado

Hy moet versigtig wees

Straight to his thighs

Dritto alle cosce

Directement aux cuisses

Yn syth ɪʀ ᴄᴏᴇꜱᴀu

Directamente a sus muslos

Vol geduik

The pre-match meal

Il pasto prima della partita

Le repas avant le match

Y ʙᴡyᴅ ᴄyn y ɢᴇᴍ

La comida anterior al partido

Die ete voor die wedstryd

**High in fibre,
low in cholesterol**

*Ricco di fibre,
povero in colesterolo*

Riche en fibres, pauvre en cholestérol

Yn ychel mewn ꜰꜰɪʙʀ ɪꜱel mewn colestenol

Alto en fibra, bajo en colesterol

Baie vesel, min cholesterol

THE COMMENTARY BOX

'Naturally, as commentators,
we have to remain strictly impartial.'

We have to remain strictly impartial

Dobbiamo rimanere assolutamente imparziali

Nous devons rester strictement impartiales

Rydyn yn gorfod aros diduedd

Tenemos que permanecer imparciales

Ons moet streng onpartydig bly

The commentary box

La tribuna dei radiocronisti

La cabine des commentateurs

Y bocs esboniad

La cabina de transmisión

Die kommentaar-hok

Expert analysis from...

Un'analisi approfondita da...

Une excellente analyse de la part de...

dadansoddwr proffesiadol oddiwrth...

Análisis experto de...

Gesaghebbende ontleding van...

Welcome back to Murrayfield

Benvenuti nuovamente a Murrayfield

Bienvenue de nouveau à Murrayfield

Croeso nol i murrayfield

Bienvenidos nuevamente a Murrayfield

Welkom terug by Murrayfield

HALF-TIME AT THE BAR

'I don't know which is harder - scoring a try,
or trying to get a pint!'

I don't know which is harder

Non so cosa sia più difficile

Je ne sais pas ce qui est le plus difficile

Rwy ddim yn gwybod beth yw mwy galed

No sé qué es más difícil

Ek weet nie wat die moeilikste is nie

I'm trying to get a pint!

Sto cercando di prendermi una birra!

J'essaie de me faire servir une bière!

Rwyn trial cael peint!

¡Procuro conseguir una cerveza!

Ek probeer 'n bier kry!

Two pints of beer please

Due birre, per favore

Deux bières, s'il vous plaît

Dwy peint o cwrw, gwelwch yn dda

Dos cervezas, por favor

Twee biere, asseblief

How much?

Quanto?

C'est combien?

Faint yw e?

¿Cuánto es?

Hoeveel?

ON THE TOUCH-LINE

'I'd love to help out,
but I've got to keep my eye on this rowdy bunch.'

**I'd love
to help out, but...**

Vorrei tanto dare una mano,
ma…

Je voudrais bien aider, mais…

Byddwn i yn caru helpu
maes, ond…

Me encantaría ayudar, pero…

Ek sal graag help,
maar…

**Rowdy
bunch**

Banda attaccalite

Un groupe de chahuteurs

swyn llyð

Un montón de alborotadores

Rumoerige klomp

The stretcher is on the pitch

La barella è in campo

Le brancard est sur le terrain

mae'r elorwely ar y cae

La camilla está en la cancha

Die draagbaar is op die veld

Friendly rivalry

Cordiale rivalità

Une rivalité amicale

Cydymgais cyfeillgar

Rivalidad amistosa

Vriendskaplike mededinging

THE CROWD

'You'd better get those glasses seen to – it wasn't a try ,
it's a streaker.'

**Your team
has just lost**

*La tua squadra ha
appena perso*

Votre équipe vient de perdre

Mae eich tîm wedi colli

Acaba de perder tu equipo

Jou span het nou
net verloor

**Get
those glasses
checked out!**

Fatti controllare la vista!

Allez faire vérifier vos lunettes!

Cael gwdraid hynny i ar chwilia allan!

¡Límpiate los lentes!

Laat kyk na jou bril!

The supporters will go home happy tonight

Stasera i tifosi andranno a casa felici

Ce soir les supporters vont rentrer contents

Bydd y cefnogwyr yn mynd garteref
heno yn hapus

Esta noche la hinchada se irá a casa contenta

Die ondersteuners sal gelukkig gaan slaap

**Followed their team
through thick & thin**

Hanno sostenuto la loro squadra fedelmente

Ils ont suivi l'équipe pour le meilleur et le pire

Roedd y cefnogwyr wedi mynd gyda'r tim trwy
denaula drwehus

Siguieron a su equipo en las buenas y en las malas

By hul span gestaan

THE CROWD

'That comment you made when he dropped the ball
- I think he may have heard you.'

He dropped the ball

Ha fatto cadere la palla

Il a fait tomber le ballon

Roedd e wedi colli bêl

Se le cayó la pelota

Hy het die bal laat val

I think he may have heard you

Penso che ti abbia sentito

Je pense qu'il a pu vous entendre

Rydw i yn credi y fod e wedi clywed chi

Creo que te debe haber escuchado

Ek dink hy't jou gehoor

That comment you made

Quel commento che hai fatto

Ce commentaire que vous avez fait

hwnna roedd e ti wedi dwead

Ese comentario que hiciste

Daai kommentaar wat jy gelewer het

Player attacks fan shock!

Sconvolgente: giocatore assale tifoso!

Un joueur attaque un supporter!

Chwaraewr wedi atacio sioc cefnogwyr!

El shock de un jugador que ataca a un hincha!

Speler val ondersteuner-skok aan!

THE CROWD

'Do you suppose <u>he</u> knows which side he's on?'

I'd cheer him all the way
Farei continuamente il tifo per lui
Je le soutiendrais jusqu'au bout
Byddwn i yn fe gyd lloni ar ffordd
Lo alentaría en todo momento
Ek sou vir hom hande klap

Make out which side he's on
Capire da che parte sta
Essayez de voir de quel côté il est
Gwneud mas pa ochr mae e arno
Darse cuenta de qué lado está jugando
Besluit aan watter kant hy speel

The pitch is waterlogged
Il campo è allagato
Le terrain est inondé
Maer cae llawn dwr
La cancha está inundada
Die veld is sopnat

Appalling conditions
In stato pietoso
Des conditions exécrables
Cyflwr ofnadwy
Pésimas condiciones
Skokkende toestande

GOING TO THE MATCH

'I'm going to be in deep trouble when I get home,
and the wife's mother finds out I'm wearing her hair!'

I'm going to be in deep trouble

Sarò nei guai fino al collo

Je vais avoir de gros problèmes

Rydw i yn mynd i cael trwbwl dufwrn

Voy a estar en grandes problemas

Ek gaan in groot moeilikheid wees

I'm wearing her hair

Sto indossando la sua parrucca

Je porte ses cheveux

Rwyn gwisgo ei gwallt hi

Llevo su peluca

Ek dra haar hare

Fans in fancy dress

Tifosi in maschera

Des supporters déguisés

Roedd y cefrogmr yn gwisgo dillad fansi

Hinchas disfrazados

Ondersteuners in kostuums

Wig

Parrucca

Perruque

Gwallt gosod

Peluca

Pruik

GOING HOME

'So they lost! Look on the bright side, Brian - it's a lovely day, and I think we've both caught a bit of colour...'

Look on the bright side

Guarda il lato positivo

Regarde le bon côté des choses

Edrych ar yr ochr lliwgar

Mirale el lado positivo

Kyk na die goeie kant

It's a lovely day

È una bella giornata

C'est une superbe journée

Mae en edrych yn dydd hyfryd

Es un día precioso

Dis 'n pragtige dag

We've both caught a bit of colour

Ci siamo presi entrambi un po' di tintarella

Nous avons pris des couleurs tous les deux

Mae'r ddau o ni wedi dal lliw

Los dos nos bronceamos un poco

Ons het albei 'n bietjie gebrand

So they lost!

Hanno perso, e allora!

Alors, ils ont perdus!

Felly roeddwn nhw wedi collu!

¡Así que ellos perdieron!

Toe gaan staan hulle en verloor!

'Imagine what your brother and his friends would have done to the room if their team had won!'

Armchair sportsmen

Sportivi da salotto

Des sportifs de salon

Chwaraewyr cadair freichiau

Deportistas de sillón

Rusbank-spelers

The match is on the box

La partita è trasmessa in televisione

Le match passe à la télé

Mae'r gêm ar y bocs

Pasan el partido por la tele

Die wedstryd is op die kassie

Pass the beer

Passa la birra

Passe-moi la bière

Pasiwch y cwrw

Pasame la cerveza

Gee die bier aan

Turn the volume up

Alza il volume

Monte le volume

Trowch y swn i'r llan

Sube el volumen

Maak bietjie harder

English	Italian	French
Referee	Arbitro	L'arbitre
Touch Judge	Giudice di linea laterale	L'arbitre de touche
Full-back	Tre quarti estremo	L'arrière
Wings	Tre quarti ala	Les ailiers
Centres	Tre quarti centro	Les centres
Outside-Half	Mediano di apertura	Le demi d'ouverture
Scrum-Half	Mediano di mischia	Le demi de melée
Prop	Pilone	Le pilier
Hooker	Tallonatore	Le talonneur
Second row	Seconda linea centro	La deuxième ligne
Wing Forward	Terza linea	L'ailier
Number 8	Terza linea centro	Le numéro huit
Try	Meta	Un essai
Penalty	Calcio di punizione	Un pénalité
Drop Goal	Gol su drop	Le drop-goal
Conversion	Trasformazione	La transformation
Free kick	Tiro libero	Un coup franc
Knock-on	Pallone in avanti	Un en-avant
Ruck	Mischia spontanea	Une melée ouverte
Maul	Maul	Un maul
Scrum	Mischia	Une melée
Drop-Out	Rimessa in gioco	Un renvoi aux 22 mètres
Line-Out	Rimessa laterale	La touche
Dummy	Finta	La feinte
Sideline	Linea laterale	La ligne de côté/touche
Goal Line	Linea di meta	La ligne de but
Dead Ball Line	Linea di pallone morto	La ligne de ballon mort
The 22 (22 metre line)	Linea dei 22m	Les vingt-deux
Goal Posts	Porta	Les poteaux
Half-way line	Linea di metà campo	La ligne médiane